Wise Words
and
Ridiculous Rhymes

Written by Laura Bartolucci
Illustrated by Maris Shepherd

Logan,

Wishing you wisdom & laughter!

Love,

Mrs. Bartol.

Wise Words and Ridiculous Rhymes
Copyright © 2013

Poopoonunu Productions by Laura Bartolucci

Illustrated by Maris Shepherd
Editing Support Provided by Susan Bartolucci and Mark Gutierrez
ISBN: 978-1494286798

This book is dedicated to all my former students,
many of whom over the years encouraged me
to publish these poems.
I finally did it!
Thanks for your votes of confidence!

Perspective

You've all heard the story of Sweet Dorothy Gale
who spent some time here in Oz.
She got caught in a twister
and squashed my poor sister
with no known or probable cause.

Then she took the red slippers from my sister's feet,
though they should have been passed down to me.
I can't help but feeling,
that's actually stealing,
and the one who is "wicked" is me?

Next, she goes to the wizard who gives her the task
of procuring the broom of "Yours Truly."
Now it's me that she's after,
and that spells disaster.
Can you blame me for acting unruly?

Since you've heard the story, you know how it ends.
You know the sad card I was dealt.
That mean, evil plotter
splashed me with water
and watched as I started to melt.

Then Dorothy's triumphant and goes on back home,
while I'm just a puddle of goo.
I should have dispatched her,
squashed her and smashed her,
her and her little dog, too!

Cockroach Stew

Let me plead a case for the cockroach
who's detested, spurned, and feared.
In our house he's an honored guest,
admired and revered.

He's creepy and he's crawly,
I'll admit that's very true.
But we welcome every cockroach in,
for they make a tasty stew!

I used to push my bowl away
when Mother served me stew.
Till by accident a roach dove in,
which added something new.

Twelve cockroaches per potful
improves the stew a bunch.
They add a spicy flavor
and a bit of extra crunch!

We've tried using other critters,
throwing each into the pot.
But earthworms are too juicy
and red ants make it too hot.

Flies make it too salty,
and termites, they're too sweet,
and when it comes down to nutrition,
the roach is hard to beat!

So next time you spot a cockroach,
do not scream and fuss a lot.
Simply scoop him up and toss him
in your mother's stewing pot.

Getting Into Books

One night as I was reading favorite stories in my bed,
I found myself within the very scene that I'd just read.

The walls of my own room had simply vanished somewhere yonder
and throughout the pages of my book I soon began to wander.

And who should I encounter as I started on my walk?
None other than the giant from Jack's mighty, magic stalk!

He picked me up and placed me with one great and gentle sweep,
in a castle where a lovely girl was lying fast asleep.

I watched in awe as a handsome prince bent to break the spell,
then we simply exchanged handshakes as a way to say farewell.

I wandered on until I found a delicious banquet feast
and seated at the other end was a most atrocious beast!

Since I knew about this story, I decided not to stay,
grabbed a ride upon Old Mother Goose and continued on my way.

Then I had a conversation with a girl all dressed in red.
She was headed for her grandma's, but she met a wolf instead.

I should have warned her not to talk to strangers in the wood,
but if she doesn't mind her mother, then I'm sure it'd do no good.

Last thing that I remember, though it isn't very clear,
is conversing with a cat who would smile, then disappear.

Next thing I know, I'm back in bed. Mother's turning off the light.
She comes to kiss and tuck me in and tell me to "sleep tight."

She says, "I'm glad you're into books," as she bends to kiss my cheek.
If she only knew the truth within those words she chose to speak!

Emily and the Egg

Emily had always been a pretty normal kid.
So when she sat upon that egg, folks thought she'd flipped her lid.
They knew her plan to hatch the egg would certainly be foiled,
for the egg on which she sat
had been recently hard-boiled.

But Emily was determined that she'd bring the egg to life,
even if it cost her added stress and added strife.
She took it everywhere she went, for care it did not lack,
as anxiously she waited
for that anticipated "crack".

Her mom said, "You've gone batty if you think it can be hatched.
Why couldn't it be a teddy bear to which you are attached?
It really is unnatural to on an egg be hooked,
or to try to hatch an egg
which you know is fully cooked!"

But Emily didn't listen. They could not intimidate.
She was serious about her job, which was to incubate.
Then one day there came a scratch,
in amazement people stood,
and Emily's chick broke through the shell
'cuz she believed it would!

The Odd Couple

A rhinoceros and an ostrich fell in love when first they met,
not realizing all the teasing their relationship would get.

Said the rhino's friends, "She's clumsy and quite ugly for a bird.
Together you look awkward and to say the least, absurd!"

"Whatever do you see in her?" his buddies did entreat.
"Her neck's too long, her eyes they bulge, and she has the biggest feet!"

Her friends were no better. They teased, "Dear, be you forewarned,
for when he tries to kiss you, he will stab you with his horn!"

"And have you noticed he's quite bald? No feathers does he sport.
We'll never understand why it is he you choose to court."

"The worst thing, as you'll surely note, his eyes are placed too low,
which lends the look, to ice the cake, that he is dull and slow."

But when each looked at the other, despite the laughs and taunts,
they saw only true companions; fun and loving confidants.

So remember as you pass through life, the message this does impart:
Real beauty lies within to be discovered by the heart.

The Privileges of Old Age

My grandpa came to visit
and it isn't hard to see
my folks put up with lots of things
they *never* would from me.

When *I* play my music loud,
my parents raise a stink.
But Gramps can blast the T.V.
and no one will even blink.

He also can be mean and cross
and still they treat him kind.
He never has to take a bath,
unless he's so inclined.

If Gramps won't eat what's on his plate,
my parents don't harass.
And no one even bats an eye
when Grandpa passes gas!

I can't wait until I'm old and gray
and grouchy like a bear.
I'll spend all day around the house
in just my underwear.

It's safe to say that life will be
much easier by far,
'cuz you never have to brush your teeth,
just soak them in a jar.

But best of all I'll get to say
exactly what I feel,
without the risk of getting sent
to bed without a meal!

Domino

Domino wasn't like the other zebras in the herd.
Because of this, they ridiculed and made him feel absurd.
You see, instead of stripes like the other zebras gots,
Domino was black as coal and covered with white spots.

Because he was so different, he would never quite fit in;
forever, on the outside, much to his chagrin.
While the other zebras pranced and played, Domino stood alone.
They could not accept him. No friendship was he shown.

Then one day a circus man came looking for a star;
someone who would draw a crowd of people near and far.
He took one look at Domino and knew he'd found his prize.
So he loaded him up quickly, and they left without "good-byes."

Now people come from miles around to see young Domino.
They marvel at his beauty and they pay to see his show.
He's proud of being different, for that's what earned him fame.
This world would sure be boring, if we were all the same!

Holiday Twist

If Christmas was a summer,
not a winter holiday,
Santa'd have a team of camels
'stead of reindeer for his sleigh.

Though the reindeer do a perfect job
in blizzards, snow and sleet,
camels would for certain
do much better in the heat.

Santa'd have to make some changes,
he would have to substitute
a pair of bright Bermuda shorts
for that heavy flannel suit.

Though at first he would feel silly,
and he'd look a little weird,
the sunshine would force Santa
to shave off his long, gray beard.

There'd be no roasting chestnuts,
for there'd be no open fires.
For Santa we'd leave lemonade
which summer thirst requires.

On songs that mention winter's white,
we'd have to place a ban.
And sing instead of catching rays
for a deep, dark Christmas tan.

Though it may seem completely different,
and to say the least quite strange,
in the end it wouldn't matter,
for the meaning doesn't change.

An Anteater Went for Pizza

An anteater went for pizza
and I must admit the truth,
as he sat and ate that pizza,
he looked like quite a goof.

The mess he made was bigger
than my baby brother Tom,
who throws food around the kitchen
and spits carrots at my mom!

But the anteater had a problem
'cuz he's used to eating ants.
There was pepperoni on his head
and sausage on his pants.

The waitress was appalled at him,
the manager gave a shout.
Though he'd paid like all others,
I was afraid they'd throw him out!

The customers sitting next to him
began to feel sick,
so they gobbled down their dinners
and they left the restaurant quick.

Me, I just felt sorry for him,
for pizza's my favorite dish,
and all should savor its flavor,
be they reptile, man or fish.

By the time that he was finished
he was covered head to toes,
for you see it's near impossible
to suck a pizza through your nose.

(P.S. Anteaters don't really suck their food through their noses,
but it sure looks like that's what they're doing!)

Nosey Rosy

Rosy had the biggest ears of all within the zoo,
and she used them to catch the news that passed amongst the crew.

She never missed a story, those ears caught every one,
but hearing all the juicy stuff is only *half* the fun.

For listening's only part of it, for gossip cannot thrive
if the listener doesn't pass it on to keep the news alive.

And then, of course, it's great to add, though some think it uncouth,
extra spicy details just to liven up the truth.

Rose had quite a knack for this. She knew just what to say,
to make an average story go from boring to risqué.

Then one day she heard a tale of intrigue, lies and slurs,
and was horrified to overhear the name involved was hers!

I can't relay the message or even give the slightest hint,
for the details of the story are not suitable to print.

Let's just say that Rosy learned her lesson that fine day.
She saw things from the other side, much to her dismay.

So be careful if you choose to join in talk that is untrue,
for you may be shocked to find the latest gossip's about you!

My Pet

The kids out on the playground used to tease and call me names.
They'd never let me play with them and join in on their games.
But they've changed their tune forever, and on that I'd lay a bet.
Today I am respected 'cuz I've got a rattlesnake for a pet!

I stick him in my backpack when I leave each day for school.
And due to my new pet, my reputation's very cool.
You see, not every kid has the skill to tame a snake.
But that isn't all I've mastered and of that make no mistake.

When someone else is swinging in the swing I wish to use,
I no longer have to wait my turn, I just let my new snake loose.
I point him in the direction of the kid I wish to flee,
and immediately I get my way, the swing belongs to me!

When my teacher checks my papers and records a failing grade,
I slip my snake into her desk, prepared to make a trade.
When she opens up her drawer and Snakey's poised to strike his prey,
I say, "I'll take my pet back if you make my grade an A."

All the kids are extra nice now. They include me in each game.
I never would have guessed I'd earn such honor and such fame.
It's great to be so popular. I'm glad they finally see
that despite my faults and failings, what a great kid I can be!

Carnivorous?

Said the lioness to her cub, "Dear it's time you learned to hunt."
"For I may not always be here," she stated bold and blunt.

"You must learn to stalk and pounce so that you can catch your dinner.
But these skills come almost naturally, although you're a beginner."

So they went into the forest at the closing of the day
where they hid quite unsuspected as they waited for their prey.

The cub had been instructed and she knew she had the skill,
but when it came down to it, could she really make the kill?

Though she'd been born a carnivore and must eat meat to survive,
it's much harder to eat breakfast when your breakfast is alive!

A rabbit hopped into their view. The cub knew her time had come,
but her mouth went dry, her legs went stiff, her senses all went numb.

She didn't have the heart to attack another beast,
and there and then decided that on broccoli she would feast.

From here on out it's veggies she would seek to fill her belly;
fruit and roughage, soup and rice, bread with jam or jelly.

Now that cub is quite the healthiest in her forest habitat,
'cuz her diet's low cholesterol, with very little fat.

When I'm a Grown-Up

I can't wait till I'm a grown-up, for they've really got it made.
No more work for nothing--When I'm a grown-up, I'll get paid!

Then I'll use *my* money to buy everything I see
and never stop to question whether my dear parents would agree.

I'll eat pizza in the morning and at lunch and dinner too,
and I'll snack between each meal on the most unhealthy goo.

No one will have to tell me when it's time to go to bed.
And the words, "Go do your homework!" will forever be unsaid.

I can pick the shows I *want* to watch, instead of those I "should,"
and never have to hide my eyes just when things get good.

Adults are really lucky, and I know it will be great!
I've got so much to look forward to! I'll love it! Hey, but wait...

I guess I really haven't stopped to think this clearly through.
Perhaps to say they've got it made is not exactly true.

I forgot about the taxes that adults are forced to pay.
Plus there's so much time spent working, that there's scarcely time to play.

And when it comes to food, I believe I have mistook it,
for although they choose the menu, they also have to cook it.

And clean the house and wash the clothes and other awful stuff.
I guess to put it mildly, grown-ups have it pretty rough.

In the last analysis, I guess it's not all frills,
for when your fun is over and done, you have to pay the bills.

I didn't mean to envy them. Pretend I never did.
This grown-up stuff is not for me. I'm glad that I'm a kid!

Hearts

If hearts were made of rubber,
they'd never break in two.
They'd bounce right back when they've been hurt,
just as good as new.

If hearts were made of steel,
they'd never feel pain.
They'd withstand life's slings and arrows.
Safe and sound they would remain.

If hearts were made of plastic,
they'd be as breakable as a vase,
but it wouldn't really matter
for they'd be cheap to replace.

But alas, my friend, I fear
our hearts are made of fragile stuff.
They get broken rather easily
for they're simply not that tough.

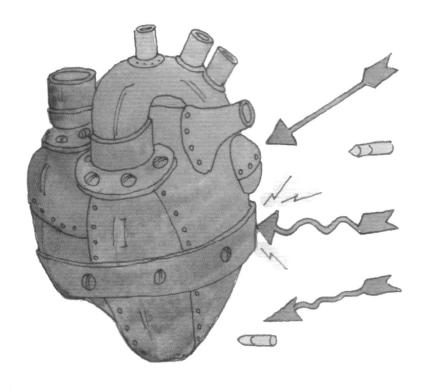

Scent-sational!

Once there was a skunk who aspired to be rich,
so she studied and she practiced to perfect her sales pitch.

Selling Avon to her neighbors was her newly chosen task.
How she fared in this endeavor, I'm sure you needn't ask.

Though her manner was quite charming, not a bottle did she sell.
For as you know a skunk is not a connoisseur of smell.

Her career was quickly finished. In the end she did relent.
For no one would buy their perfume from someone of her de-scent!

Safe

"Come out! Come out!" the critters called, "Please join us. Come and play!"
But the joey just ignored them. In his pouch is where he'd stay.

He'd heard some awful stories about the world outside his space,
and no amount of coaxing would make him show his face.

He'd heard his mother talking about the sad state of affairs,
and he didn't want to bother with a world of woes and cares.

He was safe inside his tiny room, no one could touch him there.
To venture forth from shelter was a risk he'd never dare.

But the joey didn't realize that at the same time he would miss
all the good things life could offer due to fear and cowardice.

You've got to take some chances, buckle up, give things a try,
or before you've ever lived it, life will simply pass you by.

I guess he never heard, or maybe no one had explained
the old saying we all know, "Nothing ventured; nothing gained."

There's An Aardvark in My Bathroom

There's an aardvark in my bathroom,
and I don't know why she's there.
But she's used up all my gel and mousse,
and she's blowing dry her hair.

She's put lipstick on the tip
of her long and slender nose.
She's dabbed cologne behind each ear
and put polish on her toes.

My blush is just her color,
and I admit she's looking great.
I've never seen an aardvark primp.
I guess she's got a date!

The Marriage of Rat and Cat

History has taught us that certain things don't mix;
oil and water, North and South, religion and politics.
I assume it might surprise you then to hear this tale I spread,
on a clear, cool day in autumn,
Rat and Cat were legally wed!

Since time began dear Rat and Cat have been worst enemies.
If Rat was caught by Cat, his death was quick, despite his pleas.
In fact, many a human has brought a cat into the house
for no other special reason
than to rid it of a mouse.

So when Rat and Cat first met it was for dinner, for you see,
Cat trapped Rat and licked her lips, "Ah, rodent fricassee!"
But as she prepared to gulp Rat down, she noticed something new;
his fur was soft as velvet
and his eyes a piercing blue.

They talked for hours after that and learned a thing or two
that they both had in common: for instance, going to the zoo,
or walking on the beach at night, and Saturday cartoons,
kites and book and boats and clouds,
and Elvis Presley tunes!

"How silly we have been to judge each other just by race.
To hate because our parents did makes a weak and sorry case."
To their old beliefs and biases they said, "Farewell, adieu!"
Clasped hands and hearts, walked down the aisle,
and said the words, "I do!"

There's a lesson here for each of us;
let each man stand alone,
look beyond his skin, into his heart,
before you cast a stone.

My Gum Collection*

I have a gum collection of which I am quite proud.
Whenever I display it, I stupefy the crowd.
I hand select each specimen, and though some think it crude,
each piece in my collection has assuredly been chewed.

One piece I found last summer when I went away to camp.
It was stuck beneath the shade of our cabin reading lamp.
It holds for me fond memories, all of which are good,
for I chewed it every day as we wandered through the wood.

I'm very sentimental about piece number two.
It was acquired through a swap with my girlfriend, Betty Lou.
We exchanged our chewing gum and thus exchanged a heart to heart.
We promised then that piece we'd chew until "death do us part."

This piece is quite special and unique among the rest.
I really must admit it is the piece I like the best.
If you look quite close, you'll see the imprint of the shoe
that I happened to be wearing when I stepped upon the goo.

This one is quite valuable. I'm sure it's an antique.
I found it at my grandma's when we visited last week.
It was tossed among some souvenirs inside an attic crate.
I bet my grandma chewed it back in 1898!

I have gum from 'round the country, all across this noble land,
from the mighty Mississippi, to the muddy Rio Grande.
I have gum of every color, some is old and some is new.
But wait...
I'm being greedy...
Would you like a piece to chew?

*This poem is based on a true story.
I really did collect gum when I was about six.
I made a colorful collage out of it!
It was quite a stunning piece of art.
But just so you know,
I was the only one who had chewed that gum!

The Homework Goblin

I know I had it in there. I know I had it done.
She'll be asking for it shortly since our school day has begun.

How can I begin to tell her? How can I try to explain,
that the homework goblin munched it? All my pleas will be in vain!

She never quite believes me, though I tell her every week,
that the homework goblin's clever: My assignments he does sneak.

Then he tears each into tiny scraps and chews up every bit.
Then swallows down my paper till there's nothing left of it.

I've never really seen him. And the species is quite rare.
But my homework's always, missing so I'm awfully sure he's there.

The goblin is not choosey. He'll eat work of every kind;
Social Studies, Math and Science, any homework he can find.

But I know his favorite's English, for those always disappear.
I don't think he's let me turn one in this whole, entire year.

Last month at teacher conference, Mom and Dad were shocked to see
that my grades were sharply falling, every one a C or D.

But they didn't buy it either when I told them they were chewed
by the evil homework goblin, who uses them for food.

If there's a homework goblin who resides in your desk, too,
I sure hope *your* teacher trusts you when you tell her what is true!

The Ballad of Badger and Bear

Badger and Bear had been friends for a while,
as bosom companions, they'd go out in style.
Two frolicking friends, through the forest they would run,
laughing and singing, and just having fun.

That's how it all started, but it didn't end there.
They had plenty of laughter and heartaches to share.
If either one called , they'd be there at the door,
no matter the hour, 'cuz that's what friends are for.

Badger was proud of her friendship with Bear,
for friends such as this one are special and rare.
The others were jealous of their strong, loving tie,
and Badger was sure they'd be friends till they die.

Then suddenly one day Bear just wasn't there!
Was she hiding from Badger? Did she no longer care?
"I can be bold and bristly. I must have hurt Bear,"
said Badger to Owl with a cry of despair.

Wise Owl said, "Bears hibernate in the fall.
I'm sure when she wakes up, she'll give you a call."
But time quickly passed, and with it the season.
Still no word from Bear. Badger needed a reason.

So she went back to Owl full of anger and tears.
"How could she just give up? We've been friends for years!"
Owl thought long and hard, for he sensed Badger's pain,
then he sat Badger down and he tried to explain.

"There's no way to know what Bear's feeling inside,
and it's tough to rebuild an old friendship that's died.
Friends sometimes must part and go their own way.
Friendships may flounder, frazzle, or fray.

Since Bear has been silent, there's no way to know
why this friendship of yours has failed to grow.
Move on and make new friends. Though I know you feel bad,
give thanks for the special years that you've had.
Remember the role Bear has managed to play
in helping to make you who you are today.

Metamorphosis

An ugly, fuzzy caterpillar crawled up to a nightingale
as it sat and sang a melody within its golden jail.
"You think you're so special when you sing your birdy song,
but you'll never sell a CD, for the notes come out all wrong.
You squeak and squawk and holler. It's not music to *my* ear.
If that's your only talent, you'd best find a new career."

Then she happened by a bumblebee with black and yellow rings.
"I bet you think you're better just because you have your wings.
Most people don't appreciate an insect, my dear sonny,
even though you labor long and hard to make their precious honey.
Those sorry little wings of yours won't do you any good.
You might as well just trade them in, in fact, I think you should."

She continued on her way until she came upon a rose;
the most aromatic flower in the garden, I suppose.
But the caterpillar pointed out, as critically she warned,
"You may smell pretty, Baby, but you're also full of thorns!
Though many look at you with admiration genuine,
if they pluck you from your bush, I truly hope they have thick skin!"

She was always finding major flaws no matter where she went.
When in truth it was herself in which she found her discontent.
She was jealous of the others so it took her long to see,
always finding fault with others made her less than she could be.
When she put aside her envy, cast a soulful, inward eye,
made some changes in her own life,
she became a butterfly!

Princess Lamay

"I'm tired of waiting," said Princess Lamay,
"for some handsome prince to come take me away!
I'm gorgeous! I'm loving! I'm rich and alone.
I'll go find my own prince and bring him back home!"

Her parents were shocked, the servants befuddled.
They said, "That's absurd! Your thoughts are most muddled!
That's improper conduct for a lady like you.
Behavior like that, just simply won't do!"

But Lamay wouldn't listen to the castle protest.
She packed up her things and she started her quest.
A prince she would rescue from some evil fate
and carry him homeward to make him her mate.

She hadn't gone far when she heard a weak yell.
It came from a man trapped within a deep well.
"My name is Prince Guilford. Oh, please hear my plea!"
Lamay lowered a rope and set the prince free.

"Now that you're rescued, I'll be your new wife.
We'll return to my palace and start our new life".
He'd been destined to marry sweet Martha since birth.
But he said, "Glad I met you; whatever that's worth."

So onward she traveled, her hopes were still high,
when she heard from a distance a low, mournful cry.
A handsome young prince was tied to a tree,
since bait for a dragon he was soon to be.

Lamay quickly untied him and asked for his hand
and prepared to escort him to her fatherland.
The prince said, "I'm glad to be free from my bonds,
but to tell you the truth Dear, I much prefer blondes."

Though her feelings were wounded, she wouldn't give up
till she found what she searched for, her true loving cup.

After four years of traveling, she at last found her man;
a shy, quiet prince by the name of Sir Dan.
"It took many heartaches to find you, my dear;
but a prize that's worth having takes risking I fear."

You can't wait for good things to happen to you;
when it comes to your dreams, you must make them come true!

Sharing these poems with you, is a dream come true for me.
Thanks for reading!
Laura

Laura Bartolucci is a native of Albuquerque, New Mexico. She holds a Bachelor's Degree in Education from New Mexico State University and a Master's in Gifted Education from UNM. She spent 26 exciting years teaching elementary kids, always working to inspire in them an enthusiasm for writing. These poems were written 25 years ago and have been waiting all that time to be published. They have been enjoyed by Laura's students over the years, but she is excited to finally share them with a larger audience!

Maris Shepherd lives in Albuquerque, New Mexico, where she is a prize-winning Signature Member of the New Mexico Watercolor Society. She earned a degree in Fine Arts from the University of New Mexico. Her paintings hang in hundreds of private and corporate collections in South Carolina, Texas and New Mexico. One of her latest commissions is from the Royal Family of Saudi Arabia. You can learn more about Maris at www.marisshepherd.com

This is Laura and Maris' second project together. You can order their first book, *A Cozy House for Miss Mouse*, on amazon.com.

Made in the USA
San Bernardino, CA
19 September 2014